"To all those who seek inner peace and enlightenment, this book is dedicated to you. The journey to a silent mind is not always easy, but it is worth it. May the wisdom shared within these pages guide you on your path to self-discovery and may you find the power of meditation to be a tool for transformation in your life."

THE SILENT MIND: DISCOVERING THE POWER OF MEDITATION

SHANTANU AHER

Contents

Foreword

The Silent Mind: Discovering the Power of Meditation is a powerful and transformative book that delves into the depths of the human mind and the path to inner peace. The author, Shantanu Aher, has done a masterful job of weaving together ancient wisdom and modern research to create a guide that is both accessible and profound.

As we navigate the fast-paced and often overwhelming world we live in, the practice of meditation has become more important than ever. It offers a way to quiet the mind, reduce stress, and connect with our true selves. The Silent Mind provides readers with a comprehensive understanding of the practice and its benefits, as well as practical tools to help you incorporate it into your daily life.

One of the things that I found most striking about this book is the author's ability to convey complex ideas in a clear and concise way. He has a gift for making ancient wisdom accessible to the modern reader, and his passion for the subject shines through on every page.

Whether you are new to meditation or an experienced practitioner, this book offers valuable insights and guidance. I highly recommend it to anyone seeking to deepen their understanding of the mind, and to find true inner peace and fulfillment.

Shantanu Aher's The Silent Mind is a must-read for anyone looking to improve their physical and mental well-being and to discover the true power of meditation.

Preface

The practice of meditation has been around for centuries, yet it remains as relevant today as it was in the past. In The Silent Mind: Discovering the Power of Meditation, I aim to shed light on the many benefits of meditation and how it can be integrated into our modern lives.

As I began my own journey of self-discovery and personal growth, I found that meditation was a powerful tool for me. It helped me to quiet my mind, reduce stress, and find inner peace. I was so inspired by my own experiences that I felt compelled to share the knowledge I had gained with others.

In this book, I delve into the history and science of meditation, providing readers with a comprehensive understanding of the practice and its benefits. I also share practical tips and techniques to help you incorporate meditation into your daily routine. Whether you are new to meditation or an experienced practitioner, this book offers valuable insights and guidance.

I hope that this book will serve as a guide on your own journey of self-discovery and personal growth. May you find the power of meditation to be a tool for transformation in your life.

Acknowledgements

Writing a book is a journey that requires the support and encouragement of many people. I would like to take this opportunity to express my gratitude to all those who have helped me along the way.

First and foremost, I would like to thank my family for their unwavering support and love. Their encouragement and belief in me has been a constant source of inspiration throughout the writing process.

I am also deeply grateful to my mentor and guide, who has taught me the art of meditation and self-discovery. His wisdom and guidance have been invaluable in the creation of this book.

I would like to thank my editors and proofreaders for their valuable feedback and suggestions that helped me to improve the quality of this book.

Finally, I would like to thank all the readers for taking the time to read my book and for their interest in the subject of meditation. I hope that this book will help you to discover the power of meditation and improve your physical and mental well-being.

This book is the result of the love, support, and guidance of many people, and I am deeply grateful to each and every one of them.

Prologue

In the fast-paced and often overwhelming world we live in, it can be difficult to find inner peace and quiet the mind. We are constantly bombarded with distractions and pressures, leaving us feeling stressed and disconnected from ourselves. But there is a way to break free from this cycle of chaos and find true inner peace. It is through the practice of meditation.

Meditation is a powerful tool that has been used for centuries to quiet the mind, reduce stress, and connect with the true self. But for many, the idea of meditation is shrouded in mystery and misconceptions. This book aims to demystify the practice of meditation and provide readers with a comprehensive understanding of its benefits and how to incorporate it into their daily lives.

Through the pages of this book, you will discover the history and science of meditation, learn practical tips and techniques, and gain insights into how it can be used to improve physical and mental well-being. Whether you are new to meditation or an experienced practitioner, this book offers valuable guidance and inspiration on your journey of self-discovery and personal growth.

As you begin this journey, I encourage you to keep an open mind and be patient with yourself. The path to a silent mind is not always easy, but it is worth it. May the wisdom shared within these pages guide you on your path to inner peace and self-discovery, and may the power of meditation be a tool for transformation in your life.

This book is not only about understanding the theory of meditation but also how to practice it in your daily life. It will take you on a journey from the basics of meditation to more advanced techniques, helping you to quiet your mind, reduce stress, and connect with your true self.

As you read this book, I invite you to take the time to reflect on your own experiences, and to experiment with the techniques described within these pages. Remember that the ultimate goal of meditation is not to achieve a particular state of mind, but to simply be present in the moment. So, let's begin this journey together and discover the power of a silent mind.

ONE

DEFINITION OF MEDITATION AND ITS SPIRITUAL SIGNIFICANCE

Meditation is a practice in which an individual uses a technique – such as mindfulness, or focusing the mind on a particular object, thought, or activity – to train attention and awareness, and achieve a mentally clear and emotionally calm and stable state. Meditation has been practiced for thousands of years by many different cultures and traditions for spiritual, physical, and mental well-being.

In a spiritual context, meditation is often seen as a way to connect with a higher power or a sense of inner wisdom. It can be a means of self-discovery and self-transcendence, helping individuals to gain a deeper understanding of themselves and their place in the world. Meditation can also be a way to find inner peace, clarity, and a sense of being present in the moment. Many people find that a regular meditation practice helps them to feel more grounded, focused, and centered, and to approach life with a greater sense of calm and perspective.

TWO

OVERVIEW OF THE BENEFITS OF MEDITATION

There are many potential benefits to meditation, both for the mind and body. Some of the most well-established benefits of meditation include:

Stress reduction: Meditation has been shown to help reduce stress and anxiety by calming the mind and promoting relaxation.

Improved mental clarity and focus: Meditation can help improve attention and concentration, and increase awareness and clarity of thought.

Enhanced self-awareness: Meditation can help individuals gain greater insight into their own thoughts, emotions, and behaviours, leading to a greater sense of self-awareness and self-understanding.

Improved emotional well-being: Meditation has been shown to improve mood and increase feelings of happiness, joy, and compassion.

Physical health benefits: Regular meditation has been linked to a variety of physical health benefits, including improved immune function, lower blood pressure, and reduced risk of heart disease.

These are just a few of the potential benefits of meditation – there are many others as well. It's important to note that the benefits of meditation can vary depending on the individual, and that a regular meditation practice may be more effective in producing certain benefits than others.

THREE

THE DIFFERENT TYPES OF MEDITATION PRACTICES

There are many different types of meditation practices, and what works best for one person may not be the best approach for another. Here are a few common types of meditation practices:

Focused attention meditation: This type of meditation involves focusing the mind on a specific object, thought, or activity, such as the breath, a mantra, or a candle flame. The goal is to maintain focus and attention on the chosen object while letting go of distractions.

Open monitoring meditation: This type of meditation involves maintaining an open and receptive awareness of one's thoughts, feelings, and surroundings, without judgment or attachment. The goal is to observe and acknowledge thoughts and emotions as they arise, without getting caught up in them.

Loving-kindness meditation: This type of meditation involves silently repeating phrases of loving-kindness and compassion to oneself and others. The goal is to cultivate feelings of love, understanding, and compassion towards oneself and others.

Chakra meditation: This type of meditation involves focusing on the energy centers in the body, known as chakras. The goal is to balance and align the chakras, which is believed to promote physical, emotional, and spiritual well-being.

Transcendental meditation: This type of meditation involves the use of a mantra, or a word or phrase that is repeated silently to oneself. The goal is to quiet the mind and access a state of deeper consciousness.

These are just a few examples of the many types of meditation practices that are available. It may be helpful to try out a few different approaches to see what works best for you.

FOUR

FOCUSED ATTENTION MEDITATION

Focused attention meditation, also known as concentration meditation or single-pointed meditation, involves focusing the mind on a specific object, thought, or activity, such as the breath, a mantra, or a candle flame. The goal is to maintain focus and attention on the chosen object while letting go of distractions.

To practice focused attention meditation, you can follow these steps:

Find a quiet, comfortable place to sit or lie down.

Choose an object to focus on, such as the breath, a mantra, or a candle flame.

Close your eyes or lower your gaze, and bring your attention to the chosen object.

As thoughts, emotions, or distractions arise, gently redirect your attention back to the object.

Continue to focus on the object for the duration of the meditation, being present in the moment and accepting whatever arises without judgment.

Focused attention meditation can be a useful practice for developing concentration, clarity, and calmness of mind. It can be helpful to start with short sessions (5-10 minutes) and gradually increase the duration as you become more comfortable with the practice.

FIVE

OPEN MONITORING MEDITATION

Open monitoring meditation, also known as mindfulness meditation or choice less awareness meditation, involves maintaining an open and receptive awareness of one's thoughts, feelings, and surroundings, without judgment or attachment. The goal is to observe and acknowledge thoughts and emotions as they arise, without getting caught up in them.

To practice open monitoring meditation, you can follow these steps:

Find a quiet, comfortable place to sit or lie down.

Close your eyes or lower your gaze, and bring your attention to your breath.

As thoughts, emotions, or sensations arise, acknowledge them and let them pass, like clouds in the sky.

Return your attention to the breath when you notice that your mind has wandered.

Continue to observe your experience in this way, being present in the moment and accepting whatever arises without judgment.

Open monitoring meditation can be a helpful practice for developing greater self-awareness and acceptance of one's experience, as well as reducing stress and improving emotional well-being. It can be helpful to start with short sessions (5-10 minutes) and gradually increase the duration as you become more comfortable with the practice.

SIX

LOVING-KINDNESS MEDITATION

Loving-kindness meditation, involves silently repeating phrases of loving-kindness and compassion to oneself and others. The goal is to cultivate feelings of love, understanding, and compassion towards oneself and others.

To practice loving-kindness meditation, you can follow these steps:

Find a quiet, comfortable place to sit or lie down.

Close your eyes or lower your gaze, and bring your attention to your breath.

Begin by silently repeating phrases of loving-kindness and compassion to yourself, such as "May I be happy. May I be healthy. May I be at peace."

Expand the circle of loving-kindness to include others, such as loved ones, friends, and eventually all beings.

As thoughts, emotions, or distractions arise, acknowledge them and let them pass, returning your focus to the phrases of loving-kindness.

Continue to repeat the phrases of loving-kindness for the duration of the meditation, feeling the feelings of love and compassion in your heart.

Loving-kindness meditation can be a powerful practice for cultivating positive emotions and for promoting feelings of connection and compassion towards oneself and others. It can be helpful to start with short sessions (5-10 minutes) and gradually increase the duration as you become more comfortable with the practice.

SEVEN
CHAKRA MEDITATION

Chakra meditation

Chakra meditation involves focusing on the energy centres in the body, known as chakras. The goal is to balance and align the chakras, which is believed to promote physical, emotional, and spiritual well-being.

There are seven main chakras in the body, each associated with different physical and emotional states. They are:

Root chakra (base of the spine): associated with feelings of safety, security, and stability

Sacral chakra (lower abdomen): associated with creativity, sexuality, and emotion

Solar plexus chakra (upper abdomen): associated with personal power, self-esteem, and confidence

Heart chakra (center of the chest): associated with love, compassion, and connection

Throat chakra (throat): associated with communication, self-expression, and truth

Third eye chakra (forehead): associated with intuition, perception, and wisdom

Crown chakra (top of the head): associated with spirituality, connection to a higher power, and enlightenment

To practice chakra meditation, you can follow these steps:

Find a quiet, comfortable place to sit or lie down.

Close your eyes or lower your gaze, and bring your attention to your breath.

Begin by focusing on the root chakra at the base of the spine, visualizing a spinning wheel of energy.

Slowly move up through each of the chakras, visualizing and focusing on the spinning wheel of energy at each location.

When you reach the crown chakra at the top of the head, allow your awareness to expand beyond the body.

Hold your attention on each chakra for a few moments, and imagine the energy flowing freely and smoothly.

When you are finished, take a few deep breaths and gently bring your awareness back to the present moment.

Chakra meditation can be a helpful practice for promoting balance and well-being in the body and mind. It can be helpful to start with short sessions (5-10 minutes) and gradually increase the duration as you become more comfortable with the practice.

EIGHT

TRANSCENDENTAL MEDITATION

Transcendental meditation (TM) is a specific type of meditation practice that involves the use of a mantra, or a word or phrase that is repeated silently to oneself. The goal is to quiet the mind and access a state of deeper consciousness.

TM was introduced to the West in the 1960s by Maharishi Mahesh Yogi, and has since gained millions of practitioners around the world. It is a simple and effortless technique that is said to allow the individual to experience a state of restful alertness and to access the deepest levels of consciousness.

To practice TM, you can follow these steps:

Find a quiet, comfortable place to sit or lie down.

Close your eyes or lower your gaze, and bring your attention to your breath.

Choose a mantra, a word or phrase that has personal meaning for you.

Gently repeat the mantra to yourself, either out loud or silently in your mind.

Allow the mantra to effortlessly take you deeper into a state of relaxation and inner calm.

When you are finished, take a few deep breaths and gently bring your awareness back to the present moment.

TM is typically taught by certified teachers in a course that includes personal instruction and follow-up support. It is recommended to learn TM from a certified teacher in order to ensure proper technique and to receive support in establishing a daily practice.

NINE

ZEN MEDITATION

Zen meditation, also known as zazen, is a form of meditation that is practiced within the Zen Buddhist tradition. It involves sitting in a comfortable and upright position, and focusing the mind on the present moment, without judgment or attachment. The goal is to cultivate a clear and peaceful state of mind, and to achieve a deeper understanding of one's true nature.

To practice Zen meditation, you can follow these steps:

Find a quiet, comfortable place to sit, either on a cushion or in a chair with your feet firmly planted on the ground.

Sit with your back straight and your eyes lowered, gazing downward at a 45-degree angle.

Place your hands on your lap or on your knees, with your palms facing up or down.

Bring your attention to your breath, and let go of any thoughts or distractions.

When you notice that your mind has wandered, gently redirect your attention back to the breath.

Continue to sit and focus on your breath for the duration of the meditation, accepting whatever arises without judgment.

Zen meditation can be a helpful practice for developing a sense of inner peace, clarity, and balance. It can be helpful to start with short sessions (5-10 minutes) and gradually increase the duration as you become more comfortable with the practice.

TEN
TAOIST MEDITATION

Taoist meditation is a form of meditation that is practiced within the Taoist tradition, which originated in ancient China. The Taoist tradition emphasizes living in harmony with the natural flow of the universe, known as the Tao. Taoist meditation practices are diverse and varied, and can include techniques such as qigong, visualization, and inner alchemy.

One common Taoist meditation practice is qigong, which involves gentle physical movements, deep breathing, and visualization to cultivate and balance the flow of qi (life energy) in the body. Qi is believed to be the vital energy that animates all living things, and maintaining a healthy flow of qi is considered essential for physical, emotional, and spiritual well-being.

To practice qigong meditation, you can follow these steps:

Find a quiet, comfortable place to sit or stand. It can be helpful to choose a location with fresh air and natural surroundings, such as a park or a garden.

Begin by taking a few deep breaths, and allow yourself to relax and let go of any tension.

Gently move your body in a way that feels natural and comfortable, paying attention to your breath and the sensations in your body. Qigong movements are typically slow, fluid, and graceful, and may involve stretching, waving, or circular motions.

ELEVEN
VIPASSANA MEDITATION

Vipassana meditation is a form of insight meditation that originated in ancient India. The goal of Vipassana meditation is to gain insight into the true nature of reality, by developing a deep understanding of the impermanent and interconnected nature of all things.

To practice Vipassana meditation, you can follow these steps:

Find a quiet, comfortable place to sit or lie down.

Close your eyes or lower your gaze, and bring your attention to your breath.

Notice the sensations of the breath as it moves in and out of the body, and try to maintain a focus on the present moment.

As thoughts, emotions, or distractions arise, acknowledge them and let them pass, returning your focus to the breath.

Continue to observe your experience in this way, being present in the moment and accepting whatever arises without judgment.

Vipassana meditation can be a helpful practice for developing greater awareness, understanding, and acceptance of one's experience. It can be helpful to start with short sessions (5-10 minutes) and gradually increase the duration as you become more comfortable with the practice. Vipassana meditation is typically taught in retreat settings, where students have the opportunity to practice for longer periods of time under the guidance of a teacher.

TWELVE

History of Meditation

Meditation has a long and rich history, and its origins can be traced back to ancient civilizations around the world. Evidence of meditation practices has been found in ancient cultures such as India, China, Greece, and Egypt.

In ancient India, meditation was considered a means to gain self-knowledge and liberation from suffering, and was practiced within the Hindu and Buddhist traditions. The Vedas, the oldest scriptures of Hinduism, contain references to meditation, and the Upanishads, a collection of philosophical texts, contain teachings on the nature of the self and the path to liberation through meditation. The Hindu tradition includes a wide variety of meditation practices, including the repetition of mantras, visualization, and the cultivation of specific virtues. In Buddhism, meditation is considered an integral part of the path to enlightenment, and the Buddha himself was said to have attained enlightenment through meditation. The Buddhist tradition includes a wide variety of meditation practices, including mindfulness meditation, loving-kindness meditation, and concentration meditation.

In ancient China, meditation was viewed as a way to cultivate qi (life energy) and to achieve a state of harmony and balance. The Chinese practice of qigong, which combines meditation, movement, and breath control, has a long history and is still practiced today. The Chinese philosopher Lao Tzu, the founder of Taoism, also taught the importance of cultivating inner stillness and cultivating a state of "wu wei," or non-doing, through meditation. Taoist meditation practices include qigong, visualization, and inner alchemy.

In ancient Greece, meditation was practiced as a means to cultivate virtue and wisdom. The philosopher Plato wrote about the practice of "dianoia," or contemplation, as a way to gain insight into the nature of reality. The philosopher Aristotle also wrote about the benefits of "contemplative living," or the practice of dwelling on philosophical truths in order to achieve a state of inner peace and understanding.

In Judaism, meditation was practiced as a means to connect with God and to understand the Torah. The Jewish tradition includes various forms of meditation, including the recitation of mantras, the repetition of prayers, and the contemplation of spiritual teachings. The Jewish mystics, known as the Kabbalists, also developed advanced meditation techniques for attaining higher states of consciousness and a closer connection with God.

In Christianity, meditation was practiced as a way to cultivate a closer relationship with God and to understand the teachings of Jesus. The Christian tradition includes various forms of meditation, including the repetition of prayers, the contemplation of spiritual teachings, and the use of visualization.

In the modern era, meditation has gained widespread popularity as a means to reduce stress, improve physical and mental well-being, and cultivate a sense of inner peace and clarity. Many different types of meditation practices have been developed and are practiced around the world, including mindfulness meditation, loving-kindness meditation, Transcendental meditation, and Zen meditation.

Despite the diversity of meditation practices, they all share the common goal of cultivating a heightened state of awareness and a sense of inner calm and clarity.

THIRTEEN

EARLY MEDITATION PRACTICES IN EASTERN RELIGIONS

In Hinduism, meditation practices are varied and can include the repetition of mantras, visualization, and the cultivation of specific virtues. One common Hindu meditation practice is japa, which involves the repetition of a mantra or divine name as a means to purify the mind and connect with the divine. This practice is often performed using a set of prayer beads known as a mala, and can be practiced by individuals of any faith. Another Hindu meditation practice is trataka, which involves gazing at a single point or object in order to still the mind and cultivate concentration. This practice is believed to help improve concentration and clarity of mind, and can be practiced using a candle flame, an image of a deity, or any other point of focus. Hindu meditation practices can be practiced by individuals of any faith and are not necessarily tied to any particular religious beliefs.

In Buddhism, meditation is considered an integral part of the path to enlightenment. The Buddha himself was said to have attained enlightenment through meditation, and the Buddhist tradition includes a wide variety of meditation practices. Mindfulness meditation, which involves paying attention to the present moment without judgment, is one of the most widely practiced forms of Buddhist meditation. This practice involves bringing one's attention to the breath, bodily sensations, or other present-moment experiences, and is believed to help cultivate greater awareness and understanding of the impermanent and interconnected nature of all things. Loving-kindness meditation, which involves cultivating feelings of love and compassion towards oneself and others, is another popular form of Buddhist meditation. This practice involves silently repeating phrases that express well-wishes and compassion, and is believed to help cultivate a more open and loving heart. Concentration meditation, which involves focusing the mind on a single object or sensation, is also practiced in the Buddhist tradition. This practice involves focusing the mind on a single point of focus, such as the breath or a mantra, and is believed to help improve concentration and mental clarity.

In Taoism, meditation is viewed as a way to cultivate qi (life energy) and to achieve a state of harmony and balance. The Chinese practice of qigong, which combines meditation, movement, and breath control, has a long history and is still practiced today. Qigong practices involve movements that are slow, graceful, and mindful, and can include standing, sitting, or lying down postures. The Chinese philosopher Lao Tzu, the founder of Taoism, also taught the importance of cultivating inner stillness and cultivating a state of "wu wei," or non-doing, through meditation. Taoist meditation practices include qigong, visualization, and inner alchemy. Visualization practices involve creating mental images or scenarios as a means of cultivating a sense of inner peace and clarity.

FOURTEEN

THE SPREAD OF MEDITATION TO THE WEST THROUGH SPIRITUAL TEACHERS AND TRAVELLERS

The spread of meditation to the West can be traced back to the late 19th and early 20th centuries, when Eastern spiritual teachers and travellers began to visit and teach in the West. These early teachers and travellers played a key role in introducing Eastern spiritual practices, including meditation, to the West, and their teachings and writings continue to influence the practice of meditation in the modern era.

In the late 1800s, Swami Vivekananda, a Hindu monk, travelled to the United States and introduced the teachings of Hinduism and Yoga to a Western audience. Swami Vivekananda was a key figure in the introduction of Hinduism and Yoga to the West, and his teachings and writings played a significant role in popularizing these practices in the Western world. In the 1930s, Paramahansa Yogananda, another Hindu monk, travelled to the United States and introduced the practice of Kriya Yoga, which combines meditation, breath control, and physical postures, to a Western audience. Paramahansa Yogananda's teachings and writings on Kriya Yoga and meditation have had a lasting impact on the practice of meditation in the

West.

In the 1950s, the Tibetan Buddhist teacher Chogyam Trungpa introduced the practice of Tibetan Buddhism and meditation to the West. Chogyam Trungpa was a key figure in the transmission of Tibetan Buddhism to the West, and his teachings and writings on meditation and mindfulness have had a significant influence on the practice of meditation in the Western world. In the 1960s, the Vietnamese Zen master Thich Nhat Hanh introduced the practice of Zen Buddhism and mindfulness meditation to the West. Thich Nhat Hanh's teachings and writings on Zen Buddhism and mindfulness meditation have been widely influential and have helped to popularize these practices in the West.

In the decades that followed, meditation and mindfulness practices have been embraced by people of all faiths and backgrounds, and have been integrated into mainstream Western culture as a means to reduce stress, improve physical and mental well-being, and cultivate a sense of inner peace and clarity. Today, meditation is practiced by millions of people around the world and has become a widely accepted and respected practice for promoting well-being and cultivating inner peace. Many different types of meditation practices have been developed and are practiced in the West, including mindfulness meditation, loving-kindness meditation, Transcendental meditation, and Zen meditation, and these practices continue to evolve and adapt to meet the needs of practitioners in the modern world.

FIFTEEN

THE SCIENTIFIC STUDY OF MEDITATION AND ITS EFFECTS ON THE BRAIN AND BODY

In recent years, the scientific study of meditation and its effects on the brain and body has gained widespread attention, and a growing body of research suggests that meditation may have a range of physical and mental health benefits.

One area of research that has garnered significant attention is the study of the effects of meditation on the brain. Neuroimaging studies using techniques such as functional magnetic resonance imaging (fMRI) and positron emission tomography (PET) have suggested that meditation may lead to changes in brain structure and function. For example, some studies have found that regular meditation practice is associated with an increase in the thickness of certain areas of the cerebral cortex, including the prefrontal cortex and the insula, which are involved in attention and sensory processing. Other studies have found that meditation may alter the brain's response to stress and may help to reduce the activation of the stress response system, potentially leading to reduced feelings of stress and anxiety.

In addition to its effects on the brain, research has also explored the potential benefits of meditation on various physical health outcomes. Some studies have suggested that meditation may help to reduce blood pressure and improve sleep, which are both risk factors for heart disease. Other studies have suggested that meditation may have benefits for conditions such as chronic pain, irritable bowel syndrome, and anxiety disorders.

Overall, the research on the effects of meditation on the brain and body suggests that meditation may have a range of physical and mental health benefits, and that it may be an effective tool for promoting well-being and reducing stress. However, it is important to note that the evidence for the specific benefits of meditation is still emerging, and more research is needed to fully understand the mechanisms underlying these effects and to determine the optimal way to use meditation as a therapeutic intervention.

SIXTEEN

HOW TO START A MEDITATION PRACTICE

Meditation is a simple and effective way to reduce stress, improve mental and physical well-being, and cultivate a sense of inner peace and clarity. If you're interested in starting a meditation practice, there are a few steps you can take to get started:

Choose a comfortable, quiet place to meditate. Find a place that is free from distractions, such as a quiet room or a peaceful outdoor location. It's important to create an environment that is conducive to meditation, so try to find a place where you won't be disturbed by noises or other distractions. Make sure you are comfortable and won't be interrupted during your meditation.

Set aside a specific time for meditation. Choose a time of day that works best for you, whether it's first thing in the morning, during your lunch break, or before bed. Consistency is key, so try to meditate at the same time every day. This can help to establish a regular meditation routine and make it easier to stick with your practice.

Find a comfortable position. There are many different positions you can use for meditation, including sitting, lying down, or even walking. Choose a position that is comfortable for you and allows you to remain alert and focused. If you're sitting, try using a cushion or chair to support your back. It's important to be comfortable, but you also want to avoid getting too comfortable, as this can lead to drowsiness.

Focus your attention. One of the most common ways to meditate is to focus your attention on your breath. Simply pay attention to the sensation of your breath as it moves in and out of your body. If your mind wanders, gently redirect your attention back to your breath. It's normal for your mind to wander, and it's okay if you struggle to stay focused. Don't get discouraged or frustrated, simply bring your attention back to your breath whenever you notice your mind has wandered.

Start small. Meditation is a skill that takes time and practice to develop, so start with short sessions and gradually increase the length of your meditation as you become more comfortable. You might start with just a few minutes of meditation and gradually work your way up to longer sessions. It's important to be patient and not to expect too much from yourself in the beginning. With time and practice, you'll find that it becomes easier to maintain your focus and cultivate a sense of inner peace.

Experiment with different types of meditation. There are many different types of meditation, including mindfulness meditation, loving-kindness meditation, and concentration meditation. Each type of meditation has its own unique benefits and techniques, so it's worth experimenting with different types to see which one works best for you. Some people find that they prefer one type of meditation over others, while others enjoy a combination of different practices.

Be patient. Meditation is a skill that takes time and practice to develop, so don't get discouraged if you find it difficult at first. It's normal for your mind to wander, and it's okay if you struggle to stay focused. With time and practice, you'll find that it becomes easier to maintain your focus and cultivate a sense of inner peace. It's important to be patient and not to expect too much from yourself in the beginning. With regular practice, you'll find that meditation becomes an integral part of your daily routine, and you'll be able to experience the many benefits it has to offer.

Incorporating meditation into your daily routine can be a powerful way to reduce stress, improve mental and physical well-being, and cultivate a sense of inner peace and clarity.

SEVENTEEN

THE BENEFITS OF MEDITATION

Reducing stress: One of the most well-known benefits of meditation is its ability to reduce stress. Stress is a normal part of life, but chronic stress can have negative effects on both physical and mental health. Meditation can help to reduce the body's stress response, which can lead to lower levels of stress and a sense of calm and relaxation.

Improving mental clarity and focus: Meditation can help to improve mental clarity and focus by quieting the mind and helping to eliminate distractions. By practicing meditation regularly, you can improve your ability to concentrate and focus, which can be beneficial for work, school, and other activities.

Improving physical health: Meditation has been shown to have a number of physical health benefits. Some research suggests that meditation may help to lower blood pressure, reduce the risk of heart disease, and improve sleep. Other studies have found that meditation may help to reduce chronic pain, improve symptoms of irritable bowel syndrome, and boost the immune system.

Promoting emotional well-being: Meditation can also have a positive impact on emotional well-being. Some research suggests that meditation may help to reduce symptoms of anxiety and depression, and may increase feelings of happiness and well-being.

Enhancing spiritual connection: For some people, meditation is a way to connect with a higher power or a sense of spiritual purpose. By quieting the mind and focusing the attention on the present moment, meditation can create a sense of inner peace and clarity that can be beneficial for spiritual growth and development.

Improving relationships: Meditation can also have a positive impact on relationships. By reducing stress and improving emotional well-being, meditation can help to improve communication and increase feelings of compassion and understanding.

Promoting better sleep: Meditation can also help to improve sleep quality. By calming the mind and reducing stress, meditation can help to relax the body and make it easier to fall asleep. Some research suggests that meditation may also help to reduce sleep disturbances and improve sleep duration.

Enhancing self-awareness: Meditation can help to increase self-awareness by providing a space for introspection and reflection. By practicing meditation regularly, you can become more aware of your thoughts, feelings, and behaviours, which can be beneficial for personal growth and development.

Improving cognitive function: Some research suggests that meditation may have a positive impact on cognitive function. For example, studies have found that meditation may help to improve memory, attention, and executive function.

Reducing anxiety: Meditation has also been shown to be an effective tool for reducing anxiety. By calming the mind and reducing the activation of the stress response system, meditation can help to reduce feelings of anxiety and increase a sense of calm and relaxation.

Improving cardiovascular health: Some research suggests that meditation may have a positive impact on cardiovascular health. For example, a study published in the Journal of the American Heart Association found that a mindfulness meditation program was associated with a significant reduction in blood pressure and an improvement in cholesterol levels among people with cardiovascular disease.

Reducing symptoms of chronic conditions: Meditation may also be beneficial for people with chronic conditions, such as asthma, cancer, and HIV. For example, a study published in the Journal of the American Medical Association found that a mindfulness meditation program was associated with a significant reduction in symptoms of anxiety and depression among people with cancer. Another study published in the Journal of Alternative and Complementary Medicine found that a mindfulness meditation program was associated with a significant reduction in symptoms of asthma among adults.

Improving physical function in older adults: Meditation may also have a positive impact on physical function in older adults. A study published in the Journal of Gerontology found that a mindfulness meditation program was associated with a significant improvement in physical function among older adults with osteoarthritis.

Improving academic performance: Meditation may also have a positive impact on academic performance. A study published in the Journal of Educational Psychology found that a mindfulness meditation program was associated with a significant improvement in test scores among high school students.

EIGHTEEN

COMMON CHALLENGES AND HOW TO OVERCOME THEM

Difficulty sitting still: One of the most common challenges in meditation is the difficulty in sitting still and remaining comfortable for an extended period of time. If you find it difficult to sit still, try using a cushion or chair to support your back, and find a position that is comfortable for you. It's also helpful to focus on your breath and bring your attention back to the present moment whenever you notice your mind has wandered.

Restlessness or boredom: Another common challenge in meditation is restlessness or boredom. If you find your mind wandering or you're feeling restless, try focusing on a specific object or sensation, such as your breath or a mantra. You can also try using guided meditations or using a meditation app to help keep you on track.

Difficulty with concentration: Some people find it difficult to concentrate during meditation, especially if they're new to the practice. If you're having trouble concentrating, try focusing on a specific object or sensation, such as your breath or a mantra. You can also try using guided meditations or using a meditation app to help keep you on track.

Distractions: It's normal to be distracted during meditation, but it can be frustrating if it's a constant challenge. If you're having trouble with distractions, try finding a quiet, peaceful place to meditate, and set aside a specific time for your practice. You can also try using guided meditations or using a meditation app to help keep you focused.

Lack of motivation: If you're having trouble finding the motivation to meditate, it can be helpful to set a specific goal for your practice, such as reducing stress or improving sleep. You can also try finding a meditation group or buddy to help hold you accountable and provide support.

Difficulty finding time: If you're struggling to find time to meditate, try incorporating meditation into your daily routine by setting aside a specific time each day for your practice. You can also try shorter meditations, such as a few minutes of mindfulness during your lunch break or before bed.

Difficulty with posture: If you're having trouble with posture during meditation, try using a cushion or chair to support your back, and find a position that is comfortable for you. It's important to be comfortable, but you also want to avoid getting too comfortable, as this can lead to drowsiness.

Discomfort or pain: It's normal to experience some discomfort or pain during meditation, especially if you're new to the practice. If you're experiencing discomfort or pain, try adjusting your posture or using a cushion or chair to support your back. It's also helpful to focus on your breath and bring your attention back to the present moment whenever you notice discomfort or pain.

Difficulty with emotions: Meditation can sometimes bring up difficult emotions, such as sadness, anger, or fear. If you're having difficulty with emotions during meditation, try focusing on your breath or using a mantra to help bring your attention back to the present moment. You can also try using guided meditations or working with a meditation teacher or therapist to help process and work through difficult emotions.

Difficulty with mental chatter: Some people find it difficult to quiet the mind and stop the mental chatter during meditation. If you're having trouble with mental chatter, try focusing on your breath or using a mantra to help bring your attention back to the present moment. You can also try using guided meditations or working with a meditation teacher or therapist to help quiet the mind and cultivate a sense of inner peace.

Overall, meditation can be a challenging practice, but it's also a rewarding one. By being patient and persistent, you can overcome common challenges and experience the many benefits of meditation. With regular practice, you'll find that meditation becomes an integral part of your daily routine, and you'll be able to experience the many benefits it has to offer.

NINETEEN

ADVANCE MEDITATION TECHNIQUES

There are many different techniques that can be used in advanced meditation, but one common approach is to focus on the breath. Here's a step-by-step guide for this technique:

Find a quiet place to sit where you will not be disturbed. It can be helpful to sit on a cushion or a chair with a straight back to support good posture.

Close your eyes and take a few deep breaths, allowing yourself to relax and become present in the moment.

Bring your attention to your breath. As you inhale, feel the air entering your nostrils and filling your lungs. As you exhale, feel the air leaving your body.

When your mind wanders, gently redirect it back to the breath. It is normal for the mind to wander, and this is not a sign of failure. Simply acknowledge the thought and then return your focus to the breath.

Continue to focus on your breath for as long as you like, allowing yourself to sink deeper into a state of relaxation and inner stillness.

When you are ready, slowly open your eyes and take a moment to reorient yourself before getting up and going about your day.

Remember that meditation is a practice, and it takes time and patience to develop the ability to focus and quiet the mind. With regular practice, you will find that you are able to go deeper into meditation and experience greater benefits.

Conclusion

The Silent Mind: Discovering the Power of Meditation is a powerful guide to the practice of meditation and its many benefits. Throughout this book, we have explored the science behind meditation, the different techniques that can be used, and the ways in which meditation can improve our physical and mental well-being. We have also looked at some of the common misconceptions about meditation and how to overcome them.

As we have learned, meditation is not about achieving a state of complete stillness or perfection. It is a practice of becoming more present, aware, and accepting of ourselves and the world around us. It is a journey of self-discovery and growth, and one that is accessible to everyone.

By committing to a regular meditation practice, we can cultivate inner peace, clarity, and balance in our lives. We can learn to navigate our thoughts and emotions with greater skill and resilience, and to live with more purpose and compassion.